I Am Not
My Circumstance

RELOADED

WORKBOOK

COLLEGE BOY
PUBLISHING

"We Breed Bestsellers"

Christian/Self-Help/Business

ISBN: 978-1-944110-28-4

Published in Dallas, TX, by College Boy Publishing. College Boy Publishing is a division of The College Boy Company & ArmaniValentino.com. To order wholesale or bulk orders of this book, please contact the publisher directly at collegeboypublishing@gmail.com or 972-383-9234.

Autographed copies of this book may be ordered directly from www.KendallTJohnson.com. Please allow up to 7-14 Business Days for delivery. Wholesale www.collegeboypublishing.com

Kendall T. Johnson is available for keynote addresses, workshops, panel discussions, consultations, and radio & television interviews by emailing collegeboypublishing@yahoo.com or by calling 870-397-1953 or 972-781-8404.

Printed in the United States of America

08 09 10 11 12 KJAV 5 4 3 2 1

I Am Not
My Circumstance

RELOADED

WORKBOOK

by
Kendall Johnson
with Armani Valentino

Public Announcement Disclaimer

The names, places, people and events in this book have been changed to protect the identity of many of the individuals mentioned and not mentioned. Any coincidences or names mentioned that match your life are coincidental. While each event is based on my own personal truth, in no way is it my intent to cause hurt or defamation of any person or business mentioned. I am thankful for each experience of my life because it has led me to understand that I am not my circumstance.

Edited by **Armani Valentino**
for College Boy Publishing, LLC

Published for Print and Digital formats by Armani Valentino
for College Boy Publishing

Cover Design by **Armani Valentino**
Cover Photo by **Zach Taylor** for KendallTJohnson.com

TABLE OF CONTENTS

SECTION 1—Page 1
Circumstances, Forgiveness, & Growth

SECTION 2—Page 13
Right Thinking, Imagination, Lack & Limitation

SECTION 3— Page 25
The Laws of the Universe

SECTION 4— Page 39
Relationships & Communication

SECTION 5—Page 49
Let Your Words Work & Defining Success

This special RELOADED workbook is designed to accompany the book, *I Am Not My Circumstance*. The purpose of the workbook is to help every individual to do the necessary work needed in order to overcome their circumstances.

In this RELOADED workbook, we'll do what we can to help you:

- Overcome your childhood & family conditioning.
- Create more success at any age.
- Rise above your present situation(s).
- Make good financial decisions.
- Choose a good mate and/or appreciate the mate you currently have.
- Preparing and accepting yourself for the GOOD that you've been hoping and praying for.
- Knowing when to let it go
- Hearing the VOICE of God
- Why your health is your wealth and should be taken more seriously.
- Getting over church hurt
- EGO & FORGIVENSS
- The LAWS you must LIVE by in order to PROSPER
- And Much more!

We would like for you take what's in the book as well as what you'll be learning and writing in this workbook, seriously. We believe that it will help you, as it has us, achieve a more balanced and fulfilled life, while helping many rise above their CIRCUMSTANCES into their I AM-ness.

With Love,
Kendall T. Johnson
Armani Valentino

I Am Not
My Circumstance

RELOADED

WORKBOOK

Section 1

Circumstances

Forgiveness

Growth

Kendall came into the world with what seemed to be circumstances that were not necessarily ideal.

Small town, in one of the poorest parts of the city, in one of the poorest states in the USA, where many places still had outside toilets or knew someone whose family used the bush. Plus she was born to a single mother, chaos in the neighborhood and household, and seemingly no hope for a better future.

What are some of the circumstances you feel may have negatively affected your childhood and adult years of life?

1. _____
2. _____
3. _____
4. _____
5. _____
6. _____
7. _____
8. _____
9. _____
10. _____

Did you know, *what you think* is what's controlling your life?
A. YES
B. NO

Do you believe that what YOU believe becomes YOUR reality?
A. YES
B. NO

Do you know that the majority of what you believe was taught to you at a time when you had barely learned to walk, talk, and eat, let alone think for yourself?
A. YES
B. NO

Have you ever wondered why you think the way you do?
A. YES
B. NO

There is a very small percentage of people actually living a very meaningful for fulfilled life. Very few people are HAPPY the majority of the time. Why do you think this is the way of life for most people?

_____

_____

_____

_____

_____

_____

_____

_____

_____

_____

_____

_____

_____

_____

_____.

Do you feel any feelings of hurt, shame, bitterness, betrayal, or resentment towards anyone from your past? Specifically your younger years of life…

A. YES
B. NO

Who hurt you?

_____

_____

Was it intentional?
A. YES
B. NO

Why do you feel you haven't been able to move forward? Did they ever apologize?

_____

_____

_____

_____.

On the following pages, write a forgiveness letter and forgive everyone who's ever hurt you in your past. The only way to move forward successfully is to sincerely FORGIVE others.

_____

_____

_____

_____

_____

_____

_____

_____

_____

_____

_____

_____

_____

_____

_____

_____

_____

I Am Not My Circumstance—RELOADED

_____

_____

_____

_____

_____

_____

_____

_____

_____

_____

_____

_____

_____

_____

_____

_____

"Until you FOR-GIVE God can not GIVE
you all that He has FOR you!"

~Armani Valentino

Growth is painful!

In general , people want to grow! Everything is either growing or dying. Many times, we are often concerned with outside presentation and growth that people can visibly see. However, the inner growth is often the most difficult and the most painful because it requires us to get uncomfortable. Much like a baby in the womb of its mother, our inner dreams, struggles, and desires for a better life cause pain and discomfort.

How do YOU perceive yourself?

(Circle all that apply)
Do you consider yourself:

Attractive	Ugly
Smart	Stupid
Victorious	Victim
Outgoing	Introverted
Confident	Uncertain
Finisher	Quitter
Honest	Manipulative
Giving	Selfish
Consistent	Wishy-Washy
Decisive	Indecisive
Healthy	Unhealthy
Forgiving	Condemning

Based on your list on the previous page, all the negative words that you circled, write them below:

_____

_____

_____

_____

_____

_____.

Now, say out loud, the following in place of each negative attribute:

I _(Your Name)_, have the right to choose to continue to be _(negative attribute)_, or focus on becoming _(positive attribute)_.

Section 2

Right Thinking

Imagination

Lack & Limitation

WHY YOU THINK
THE WAY YOU THINK

Most of our dysfunctional ways were all inherited from a family member and our earliest childhood environments. These are called generational curses or cycles.

In order to live the life that you have always dreamed, you have to get to a place where you can identify your generational cycles, face them, and conquer them!

If you remember nothing else, remember this fact, **"Thoughts are things!** And...the longer they are thought, they materialize and manifest in our lives."

As a man THINKETH in his heart, so is he. The heart represents the subconscious mind or deeply rooted ways of thinking. Thought patterns are habitual, and we are creatures of habits. It takes developing new habits in order to have a new life.

Old habits will not ever produce the new life you desire. Therefore, unless you change your mind you can't change your habits.

What are some habits you have developed throughout your life that you need to change in order have the life you desire?

_____
_____
_____
_____
_____
_____
_____
_____
_____
_____
_____
_____.

Change your thoughts and your habits... and then you'll change your life!

The Bible and other scriptures often speak of Righteous and Righteousness. There are no righteous acts without the RIGHT way of thinking preceding the action(s).

In the book, *7 Habits of Highly Effective People*, Stephen Covey presented the idea and process of Paradigms and Paradigm Shifts.

Most people are caught in a old paradigm of thought, and unless they let it go or have a paradigm shift, they will stay stuck. Stuck is one of the most common feelings clients express to counselors and coaches when wanting a more fulfilled life.

Have you ever felt STUCK?

YES or NO

We have a lot of ideas locked up in our mind that violate the laws of this universe, and that in itself poses a big problem.

Many people's thoughts are focused on who will win the next ballgame, what's happening on social media, or how can they scrape up enough money to get butt injections to look like Instagram models.

Seeking their real purpose and how to get the life of abundance that the Bible reads about, would be a much better use of time and thought space.

The other time seems to be used on worrying about negative things that have not happened. According to Dr. Norman Vincent Peale, over 90% of what we worry about never happens. So, don't worry.

I believe the most powerful force in the world is your brain/mind. Nothing else in existence has a super conscious mind as humans.

The progress of each individual is largely determined by his/her ruling mental state.

What is your dominating thought process?
NEGATIVE or **POSITIVE**

The ruling mental state of mind is what wins. We are programmed to go by our mental senses. We go by what we hear, smell, taste, or touch. Our lives are affected by all of the following:

-Perception
-The Will
-Intuition
-Memory
-Reasoning
-Imagination

The Power of Imagination

Words paint and create pictures. We think in pictures and sounds. These mental pictures create feelings, some of which are not always accurate. These feelings create states of minds and being, which materialize into real life manifestations.

You can flash your thoughts around the whole world in a matter of seconds. You can compare a thought to the speed of lightning.

For example: If you have ever been at the brink of a heated argument or you've almost got into a physical altercation... Notice how your heart starts beating fast or you start to shake. That's the power that you're mind has in the universe. Everything that you want to change outside is a reflection of what's going on, on the inside.

The mind has to be retrained, and one of the fastest ways to retrain your brain is to use your imagination. The main training that must take place is one of focus. Focus is work.

For 90 Seconds, close your eyes and imagine yourself on vacation at your favorite place or a place you'd like to go. Set yourself a timer and go!

Okay, now that you are done, take a moment write down what you felt like during your vacation.

_____

_____

_____

_____

_____

_____

_____.

Although you were imagining, you were actually creating a stimuli that if done over and over again, will begin to ATTRACT to you, the vacation you desire. It will attract the means, the ways, and situations that will allow you to take the vacation that you desire. Do this with every situation you desire and more of your desires will begin to take place for you. *Have fun* when doing this, as you just did and before long, you'll be on vacation.

About 80% - 95% of the people in the world were taught the idea of LACK. Therefore, LACK and LIMITATION continuously shows up in their lives.

Even in Christian churches and theology, the idea of lack and limitation is often subconsciously emitted from the teachers and preachers of the Gospel. Although the Christ taught that there was NO LACK IN THE KINGDOM.

Therefore, this conquest for poverty has taken over the mind of many of the followers of Christ. This should not be the case. It is a natural desire to desire the good things that God has created for his children. *You become and attract what you think most often, whether you want it or not.*

There is no lack! There are no limitations! There is plenty! Everything comes from God! Understanding where everything comes from makes it easier to obtain. In all your getting get understanding, and when you begin to think on the level of the supernatural instead of from what you see right in front of you, you will begin to attract what you begin to speak and think. What do you think you will attract?

This brings us to our next section on the LAWS of the UNIVERSE. The first of those being the LAW of ATTRACTION!

Section 3

The Laws
of the
Universe

The Law of Attraction

I have been studying The Law of Attraction since the year of 2012. The first time I was exposed to the Law of Attraction was through the movie, *THE SECRET*. This movie opened my eyes to a whole new world of possibilities! It caused me to level up my faith to a point where I had enough faith to leave my financially successful business in a city I was established, into moving to a new state thousands of miles away from family, friends, my business, and life as I knew it.

Upon moving to Orlando Florida, I had no clue of the "How?" I just knew my "Why?" This leap of faith has catapulted me into fully operating in my purpose. I am now a best-selling author, motivational speaker, a six-figure earning hairstylist, and have greatly grown my spiritual and mental life. All this happened in a matter of one-year of moving to a city where no one had ever heard of me.

I quickly began to purge myself of negative thinking, dysfunctional relationships, old habits that would continually keep me attracting negativity into my life.

After dealing with all my inner enemies, I was on the fast track to *living my best life*. This has awarded me a great business that is very profitable, more books to help others live their best life, and speaking engagements at major conferences. This is far from my life as I knew it prior to my awakening.

Like most people, I had been attracting what I didn't want. Why is this?

Energy flows where attention goes.

What you give your attention to the most is what you will attract. I have learned to ONLY give my attention to the things I want to happen.

Doing this will cause you to automatically eliminate the things you don't want.

I had to learn the difference between being real and negative. Many times, there is no difference and it usually leaves us being REAL NEGATIVE.

What are some situations you need to stop giving your energy, attention, thoughts, time, and conversation towards?

_____

_____

_____

_____

_____

_____

_____

_____

_____.

The Law of Reciprocity

The Law of Reciprocity, states that what you put out you will receive in return. It is mentioned in the Bible in Galatians as sowing and reaping.

Be not deceived; God is not mocked: for whatsoever a man soweth, that shall he also reap.

We sow in our thoughts as well as our actions. Many times, while we may not be doing a physical action, we have already done the action mentally and *it materializes in our environment because of the seeds of thought that we have sown*. Therefore, we are seeing it come back to us. And...when it comes back to us, it comes in greater abundance, good or bad. Read Luke 6:38.

The Law of Abundance

As stated previously, there *is no lack in the kingdom.* In order for lack to show up in our physical environment, there had to have been the thought of lack and limitation at some point.

There is only abundance! As a matter of fact there is often much more available than any one individual could use. As a stylist, when I was new in the industry, I had a goal of getting all the clients I possibly could and wanted the most clients.

Thank God for growth! You can't get all the clients. But, coming from the small town mentality, I subconsciously had to re-program my mind to see that I could never even handle all the clients in my city. There is <u>more than enough for all</u> individuals in almost every business and endeavor.

The Law of Use

The Law of Use is a law of the Universe that simply states, *"What you have must be used or it will be lost or taken away."*

For example, a house will go down faster if no one is living it versus having renters who aren't necessarily "ideal" tenants. Why? Houses were made to be lived in.

If you don't use your muscles, when it comes time to use them, they may not be there to support the task at hand.

Education is the same way. In my field and many others, if you're not actively doing the necessary continuing education, you will get left behind in your field and your knowledge will become outdated.

Read the story of the talents.
Luke 19:11-17

The Law of Work

In the Law of Reciprocity, is the Law of Seed Time (Sowing) & Harvest Time (Reaping), which brings us to the Law of Work. Often, when we hear preachers and teachers teach about *your blessing* or *your harvest*, there is one element that is often left out. That key element is the WORK.

The Law of Work states that ***in all work or labor there is benefit*** (Proverbs 14:23). In Seed Time, there is work in tilling the ground and planting the seeds. During Harvest Time there is work in collecting the crops as quickly as possible in order to keep the bugs, birds, and whatever else may be after your crops from getting it before you do. To rid yourself of poverty, "Make work your best friend and helper." *George S. Clason*

Work = Force X Distance

The Law of Ever-Increasing Returns

The Law of Ever-Increasing Returns works both good and bad. This law is mostly used in business, but encompasses more than money. For instance, if you plant a seed of corn, you don't get one seed of corn back; you get multiple ears of corn.

Another scripture that this correlates with is *Give and it shall be given unto you...*, which is the *Law of Reciprocity...* but the second half of this scripture explains the *Law of Ever-Increasing Returns* from a spiritual standpoint... *Good measure, pressed down, and shaken together... and running over, shall men give into your bosom.* So, if you continue an action, good or bad, the Law of Ever-Increasing Returns begins to take over and give more than you could handle, alone. Put yourself in position to take advantage of this law by becoming the best you can in your field.

The Law of Cosmic Habit Force

The Law of Cosmic Habit Force is a law of the Universe that simply states the more you do a particular action, the more permanent it becomes and harder to reverse. I first learned of this law through the writer Napoleon Hill. I have realized that many of our habits are permanently fixed.

In some cases this is good and in other cases this is not a good thing. In all industries of work, it is easier to develop good habits early on versus developing bad habits and then try to change them. It's the same way when it comes to food and exercise. The earlier in life you can develop the best eating habits, usually the better long-term health you will have created for yourself. This is also the reason why it is difficult to change your THOUGHT HABITS. The Law of Cosmic Habit Force has fixed your way of thinking.

The Law of Forgiveness

The Law of Forgiveness is one of the most important laws of the Universe. It is a law that the Creator has put in place and is in line with the Law of Grace, and many of the other laws to some extent. The law of forgiveness allows us all to be human whenever we miss the mark (the meaning of sin).

However, while we want forgiveness, I have learned that we often are not easy to GIVE forgiveness. When the law of forgiveness is not followed, we BLOCK many of our blessings.

"And when ye stand praying, forgive, if ye have ought against any: that your Father also which is in heaven may forgive you your trespasses. But if ye do not forgive, neither will your Father which is in heaven forgive your trespasses." *Mark 11:25-26*

Forgiveness is not for your enemy... It is for you. It is not a sign of weakness, but rather a sign of strength because it is an attribute of the Creator. You will either create or disintegrate.

Forgive means to let go completely! Guilt and resentment are two of the most powerful negative thoughts! Forgiveness causes everything to grow and come to you more easily. When I learned how to forgive people for real, it opened my life up for endless blessings and opportunities.

The Law of Belief

The Law of Belief is a very powerful and accurate law. Often, we believe things that are not true but through our belief, we make them so. Our level of belief in what we think, see, hear, speak or feel causes the Law of Attraction to be more effective.

What do you believe? I am a firm believer that you can tell what a person truly believes by their actions and their conversation. When both of these line up, a person is in ACTIVE FAITH.

Our beliefs are our Paradigms, as mentioned earlier. They shape who we are and the life we lead. Most of our prayers are not answered because we don't BELIEVE. The Christ said, *"Therefore I tell you, whatever you ask for in prayer, believe that you have received it, and it will be yours."* *Mark 11:24*

Section 4

Relationships
&
Communication

Relationships are one of the most important parts of life. Therefore, it is important to establish healthy relationships. You can never overcome or rise above your current circumstances without the proper relationships.

There should be consistent relationships within our lives that show our level of commitment and loyalty. In the area of *friendships*, we shouldn't switch friends every time someone doesn't do what we'd like or say what we think they should say. We need at least one friend who will be able to let us know when we're off track and out of order. There was a time in my life when I didn't want to hear what anyone had to say about anything. I am sure we've all been there. Thank God for good friends.

When it comes to our *business* relationships, we must be careful not to burn bridges because I am a living witness that doing this will cause problems that you could have easily avoided by doing things decent and in order. This usually happens when we get in our feelings and allow our EGO to make us think our role in the business relationship is more important than the other party involved. Without two or more parties, there is no relationship. You can have transactions, but not relationship. Long-term sustainability in our careers require us to create healthy mutually beneficial relationships.

When it comes to our relationships with *our mates*, we must understand that this relationship is one of the most important relationships we have other than the one with our Creator. No relationship challenges us on so many levels than relationships of the heart. It either forces us to grow (on multiple levels) or to end it.

I had a habit of running from relationship challenges because they forced me to grow. I was not enjoying the benefits of a healthy relationship because I had not matured enough to actually have a healthy relationship. Therefore, I could only attract on my *level of my belief* until I changed and prepared myself for that which I was desiring. Not only was this true for my personal relationships, but for all areas of my life. Remember, *Water seeks its own level.*

What are some relationships that have helped you to grow, spiritually, mentally, emotionally, financially, professionally?

_____

_____

_____

_____

_____

_____

_____

_____

_____

_____ .

Have you ever burned a bridge that you had to cross again?

A. YES

B. NO

If so, how did you rebuild it and what did you learn?

_____

_____

_____

_____

_____

_____

_____

_____

_____

_____

_____

_____

_____.

_____

Communication in Relationships

One of the most powerful statements when it comes to mending and/or rebuilding relationships is, *"I'm sorry! I was wrong! Hopefully you'll forgive me."*

A genuine apology can go a long ways in bridging the gap. Of course this takes communication. Today, our communication in most of our relationships seems to be dwindling.

Improper communication is ME centered. Proper communication is not. Let's take a closer look. If you break the word improper down into two words you have I'M PROPER. This is where most communication issues begin; with the mindset that what the other person has to say or is saying doesn't matter or is not proper. We all have different minds and different levels of understanding. In all thy getting, get understanding.

Again, in all thy getting, get understanding. While most people do not do so, it is in our best interest to **seek first to understand and then to be understood**. This takes practice, especially if the habit of cutting people off in the heat of conversation has been our main mode of communication. This is called miscommunication, or as I like to say MISS-communication because one or both parties *missed* one another in terms of their communication.

"There can be no connection without communication." Armani Valentino

In order for your Wi-Fi service to work, it has to be able to communicate from the server to the device. Anytime it will not connect, there is usually an error message that states something along the lines of, "Server is not communicating! Or... Windows can't communicate with the device." Until both devices are open and ready to communicate, there can be no connection.

Communication is a two person game that requires a sender and receiver. Anytime we are able to do both well, most of our relationships will be healthy and more meaningful.

How do you deal with broken relationships, whether it be with a significant other, friends, or family members?

_____
_____
_____.

Who is normally at fault when you experience losing a friend or a mate?

_____
_____
_____

What's your longest friendship? Job? Love Relationship?

1._____
2._____
3._____

Name 5 ways you can better yourself to not experience so many broken relationships.

1._____
2._____
3._____
4._____
5._____

In conclusion, moving on to a new relationship never fixes the problems from the old relationship. It adds fuel to your fire ends up creating more problems. The cycle is never ending until you begin to deal with your inner enemies.

Once you allow God to heal you in every area you hurt, you will live your full potential and be able to attract your ideal mate, career, family relations, friendships, and live a more fulfilled life.

Section 5

Let Your Words Work
&
Defining Success

Words are important! They create! They are the basis of our reality. According to scripture, the first words God spoke was, "Let there be light!" Let means: *to release from confinement.* Meaning, that the light was already there, in the darkness.

The Success and desires of your heart that you seek are already there. It is through your FAITH speech that you release it. Therefore, using the right words and knowing the meaning of words will help to create the life we desire.

Affirmations and declarations are what we need in order to trick our subconscious mind into believing that which we have not yet seen. We have to be able to **see it**, first. However, even if we can't see it, we can **say it** long enough to where we can see it in our mind and then our material reality.

"Thou shalt also decree a thing, and it shall be established unto thee: and the light shall shine upon thy ways."
~Job 22:28~

Here are a couple of affirmations that I use on a regular basis:

~

**My name is_____,
and I am attracting good, great, and wonderful things into my life!**

~

I AM so happy and grateful now that money comes to me in increasing quantities, through multiple sources, on a continuous basis, through the LAW of ATTRACTION.

Affirmations and declarations work because they eventually reach the subconscious mind and help to reprogram your current self-conversation. The conversation you have with yourself is the most important conversation you have!

Most people's conversation and self-talk is opposite of the life they truly desire.

We have all heard the words of King Solomon from Proverbs 18:21, *"Death and Life are in the power of the tongue..."* However, the second half of the scripture is usually left out. *"And those who love it shall eat of its fruit."*

We eat from the fruit of our tongue!

In Luke 6:45, ***"...For out of the abundance of the heart, the mouth speaks."*** Again, the heart represents the subconscious mind, and in order to speak different words you have to have different thoughts that are consciously programmed until they reach the heart or subconscious part of your mind.

Defining SUCCESS

You can never rise above your circumstances or sustain any level of success without defining success for yourself or without knowing and defining your own purpose. You must know what you truly desire. It makes the process of achieving it so much easier.

According to Webster online dictionary, **SUCCESS is the accomplishment of an aim or purpose.**

So, anytime you do not feel you have obtained success or consider yourself to be successful, make sure you have defined your AIM and your PURPOSE. I consider them to be pretty much the same.

A.I.M. = All Important Mission

This is your overall goal and achievement you want in life; your legacy or purpose.

Purpose is defined as, the reason for which something is done or created or for which something exists.

Do you know you're A.I.M. or Purpose?
A. YES
B. NO

What is you're A.I.M. or Purpose?

_____
_____
_____
_____
_____
_____
_____
_____
_____
_____.

FINAL THOUGHTS

You were born rich! Work from thought!

Work from the thought to the things you desire. Not from the thing to the thought.

Never allow your bank account to determine your dream or your financial status.

Follow the laws of nature (GOD) and you will not lose. Infinite resources are available to all of us. Everything in the universe will rush to your aid when you work in harmony with the laws of the Universe.

Do you wish to succeed? You must practice these laws.

Conformity is your enemy! Control your thinking! Seek and you will find!

After you complete this process and practice these principles daily. you will notice a total paradigm shift will take place, causing you to attract the life you've always dreamed of!

NOTES

NOTES

NOTES

NOTES

NOTES

NOTES

NOTES

NOTES

NOTES

NOTES

NOTES

NOTES

To order copies of this workbook or the book,
I Am Not My Circumstance

www.KendallTJohnson.com

MOTIVATES

To order other titles visit

www.CollegeBoyPublishing.com

COLLEGE BOY
PUBLISHING

"We Breed Bestsellers"

www.ingramcontent.com/pod-product-compliance
Lightning Source LLC
LaVergne TN
LVHW051815080426
835513LV00017B/1957